LEVEL UP

Motivation for
Entrepreneurs

Igniting Your
Entrepreneurial Spirit

DR LASHONDA WOFFORD

Copyright © 2025 by Dr. Lashonda Wofford

All rights reserved. No part of this publication may be reproduced, stored in a retrieval system, or transmitted in any form or by any means—electronic, mechanical, photocopying, recording, or otherwise—without prior written permission from the publisher, except in the case of brief quotations used in reviews or scholarly articles.

Publisher:

Dr. Lashonda Wofford dba All Bets On Me.
Email: info@drlashondawofford.com
Website: www.drlashondawofford.com

Cover Design: Xee Shan

Images: Provided by Dr. Lashonda Wofford

Library of Congress Control Number: 2025909977

ISBN: 979-8-9923605-3-0

First Edition, 2025

Printed in the United States of America

For permissions, bulk orders, or speaking engagements, please contact the publisher directly at the email listed above.

Dedication

To every visionary, trailblazer, and purpose-driven soul who dared to dream—even when the odds were stacked against you.

This book is for the entrepreneurs who've cried in silence, prayed for clarity, and still showed up. For the ones who've built in the dark, believed without applause, and kept going when quitting seemed easier.

You are the definition of courage. You are the blueprint for resilience.
You are the evidence that purpose always prevails.

May this book reignite your fire, remind you of your greatness, and push you to rise—even higher.

Level up. The world is waiting on your brilliance.

—Dr. Lashonda Wofford

Level Up Motivation for Entrepreneurs: Igniting Your Entrepreneurial Spirit

Success doesn't happen by accident—it's the result of clarity, courage, and relentless motivation. In Level Up Motivation for Entrepreneurs, award-winning author, purpose strategist, and leadership coach Dr. Lashonda Wofford delivers a fire-starting guide for entrepreneurs ready to break through burnout, overcome self-doubt, and rise with unstoppable purpose.

Packed with practical strategies, motivational insight, and real-world wisdom, this book is your catalyst for taking bold action, sustaining momentum, and transforming challenges into stepping stones. Whether you're launching your first business or scaling your next big idea, Dr. Wofford speaks directly to the heart of today's entrepreneur—with authenticity, faith, and fearless encouragement.

You'll discover how to:

Reignite your "why" when motivation feels low

Cultivate a success mindset rooted in vision and values

Silence your inner critic and fuel your confidence

Set purpose-aligned goals and take focused, daily action

Lead with faith, resilience, and emotional intelligence

This isn't just a motivational read—it's a call to action for entrepreneurs who are ready to level up, lead with intention, and build a business that reflects both purpose and power.

Are you ready to unlock the fire within? It's time to level up.

Dr. Lashonda Wofford

Motivation for entrepreneur's

Igniting Your Entrepreneurial Spirit

Table of Contents:

Introduction
What it Means to be an Entrepreneur
Why Choose Entrepreneurship?

Chapter 1
Discovering the Entrepreneur Within
Recognizing Your Potential

Embracing the Entrepreneurial Mindset

Chapter 2
Finding Your 'Why' The Importance of Passion

Defining Your Purpose

Chapter 3
Fueling Your Entrepreneurial Engine
Unleashing Your Creativity
Harnessing Your Energy and Drive

Chapter 4
Overcoming Fear and Doubt
Dealing with Uncertainty
Developing Resilience

Chapter 5
The Power of Vision
Setting Your Sights High
Creating a Mission Statement that Inspires

Chapter 6
The Role of Goals in Entrepreneurial Success
Goal-Setting 101
Making Your Goals SMART

Chapter 7	Turning Obstacles into Opportunities
	Embracing Challenges as Stepping Stones
Chapter 8	Building Your Entrepreneurial Tribe
	Finding Your Support Network
	Inspiring Your Team
Chapter 9	Continuous Learning and Growth
	Embracing Lifelong Learning
	Staying Current in Your Field
Chapter 10	Maintaining Balance on the Entrepreneurial Tightrope
	The Importance of Self-Care
	Balancing Work and Life
Chapter 11	Keeping the Flame Alive
	Staying Motivated for the Long Haul
	Looking to the Future: Scaling and Beyond

Introduction:

Welcome to "**The Spark: Igniting Your Entrepreneurial Spirit**" - your guide to finding and keeping the motivation necessary to succeed as a new or experienced entrepreneur.

Whether you're just beginning to consider launching a startup or you've already embarked on the entrepreneurial journey, this book is designed to provide you with the insights and strategies you need to stay inspired. Becoming an entrepreneur is not just about launching a business. It's about embracing a mindset of growth, resilience, and a never-ending pursuit of innovation.

This book will help you to discover that mindset within yourself and maintain it, no matter what challenges you face. Get ready to ignite your spark and be motivated like never before!

What it Means to be an Entrepreneur

Being an entrepreneur means much more than simply starting a business. It's a lifestyle, a mindset, and a passion. Here's what it really means to be an entrepreneur:

01
Visionary:

Entrepreneurs see opportunities where others see obstacles.

They have a unique vision of the future and the ability to recognize potential in ideas, people, and markets. They can envision a different world and are willing to take the risks necessary to turn that vision into reality.

02
Innovator:

Entrepreneurs are pioneers in their fields, always pushing the boundaries of what is possible

They are not satisfied with the status quo and constantly look for better ways to solve problems, improve systems, and deliver value.

03
Risk-Taker

Entrepreneurs understand that there's no reward without risk.

They are willing to step out of their comfort zone and take calculated risks to achieve their goals. This does not mean they are reckless; instead, they assess and manage risk, understanding that failure is often a stepping stone to success.

04
Persistent

Entrepreneurship is a journey filled with ups and downs.

Entrepreneurs are relentless in the face of challenges, never giving up on their dreams. They understand that failure is part of the journey, and they use it as an opportunity to learn, grow, and pivot.

05
Leader

Entrepreneurs inspire and motivate others to join them on their journey.

They have the ability to rally a team around a shared vision and create a culture that encourages innovation, collaboration, and mutual respect.

06
Lifelong Learner

Entrepreneurs recognize the importance of continuous learning.

They are curious and always seeking to broaden their knowledge, skills, and perspectives. They stay abreast of the latest trends, technologies, and best practices in their industry, understanding that the world is always changing, and they must adapt.

07
Resilient
The path of entrepreneurship is filled with challenges and setbacks.

Entrepreneurs are resilient, possessing the ability to bounce back from failures, learn from their mistakes, and keep moving forward.

08
Value Creator
Entrepreneurship is a journey filled with ups and downs.

Whether it's developing a revolutionary product, delivering a unique service, or crafting an exceptional customer experience, entrepreneurs are focused on creating value for their customers, their employees, their communities, and their stakeholders.

In essence, being an entrepreneur is about turning dreams into reality. It requires courage, determination, creativity, and the ability to keep going when the going gets tough. If you're ready to embrace these qualities and take on the challenges and rewards that come with them, then you're ready to embark on the exciting journey of entrepreneurship.

Why Choose Entrepreneurship?

Embarking on the entrepreneurial journey is a major decision, and it's not for everyone. However, if you're drawn to the idea of creating, innovating, and leading, entrepreneurship could be the right path for you.

Here are several reasons why people choose entrepreneurship:

01. Freedom and Independence

One of the most appealing aspects of entrepreneurship is the freedom and independence it offers. As an entrepreneur, you get to be your own boss, make your own decisions, and set your own schedule. You have the freedom to pursue your passions and create something that aligns with your values and vision.

02. Potential for Innovation

Entrepreneurship provides a platform for innovation. It allows you to create new products, services, or solutions that can make a difference in the world. If you have a unique idea and the drive to bring it to life, entrepreneurship offers the opportunity to do so.

03. Creating Jobs and Boosting Economy

Entrepreneurs play a crucial role in creating jobs and driving economic growth. By starting a business, you're not only creating job opportunities but also contributing to economic development in your community and beyond.

04. Personal Growth and Learning

The entrepreneurial journey is one of continual learning and personal growth. It pushes you out of your comfort zone, helping you to develop new skills, learn to overcome challenges, and become more resilient.

05. Financial Potential

While it's true that starting a business comes with financial risk, it also has the potential for significant financial rewards. Successful entrepreneurs have the opportunity to build wealth not only for themselves but also for their employees and investors.

06. Leaving a Legacy

Entrepreneurs have the opportunity to leave a lasting impact on the world. Whether it's a breakthrough product, a revolutionary service, or a company culture that sets a new standard for workplaces, entrepreneurship allows you to leave a legacy that extends beyond your lifetime.

07. Fulfillment

There's a deep sense of fulfillment that comes from seeing your ideas take shape and grow into a thriving business. Even more fulfilling is knowing that your business is making a positive impact on people's lives.

Entrepreneurship is a challenging yet rewarding path. It requires courage, determination, resilience, and a willingness to take risks. But for those who choose this path, the rewards can be immense, offering the chance to make a real difference, achieve personal growth, and enjoy the thrill of creating something from nothing.

Chapter 01

PART 01:
Discovering the Entrepreneur Within Recognizing Your Potential

PART 02:
Embracing the Entrepreneurial Mindset

Chapter 1:
Discovering the Entrepreneur Within Recognizing Your Potential

Entrepreneurial potential lies within all of us, but it often remains untapped because we fail to recognize it. Recognizing your entrepreneurial potential involves understanding your strengths, passions, and motivations and seeing how they can be channeled into creating something valuable.

Here are a few steps to help you recognize your potential:

01. Self-Reflection

Reflect on your interests, values, skills, and experiences. What are you passionate about? What are your strengths? What unique experiences or knowledge do you possess? This process of introspection can help you identify potential business ideas that align with who you are and what you believe in.

02. Identify Problems You Want to Solve

Entrepreneurs are problem-solvers. They look at the world and see opportunities to make it better. What problems or challenges do you see in your community, industry, or the world at large that you'd like to solve? Your desire to solve these problems is a sign of your entrepreneurial potential.

03. Assess Your Risk Tolerance

Entrepreneurship involves risk. Are you comfortable with taking calculated risks? Do you see failure as a learning opportunity rather than a setback? Your attitude towards risk and failure can indicate your potential as an entrepreneur.

04. Recognize Your Drive to Innovate

Reflect on your interests, values, skills, and experiences. What are you passionate about? What are your strengths? What unique experiences or knowledge do you possess? This process of introspection can help you identify potential business ideas that align with who you are and what you believe in.

05. Feedback from Others

Often, others can see our potential before we do. What feedback have you received from colleagues, mentors, friends, or family? Have others commented on your leadership skills, your creativity, or your perseverance? This feedback can help you recognize your potential.

06. Evaluate Your Resilience

The entrepreneurial journey is filled with challenges and setbacks. Do you have a history of bouncing back from adversity? Resilience is a key characteristic of successful entrepreneurs.

07. Reflect on Your Desire to Learn:

Entrepreneurs are lifelong learners. They're curious and always seeking to expand their knowledge and skills. If you love learning and are open to new ideas, this can be an indicator of your entrepreneurial potential.

Recognizing your potential is the first step towards becoming an entrepreneur. It can help you identify the unique contributions you can make as an entrepreneur and inspire you to take the leap into entrepreneurship. Remember, every successful entrepreneur started with a spark of potential. Recognize yours, nurture it, and watch it grow.

Chapter 1:
Discovering the Entrepreneur Within Embracing the Entrepreneurial Mindset

The entrepreneurial mindset is more than a set of traits or skills; it's a way of thinking and behaving. It's about seeing opportunities instead of obstacles, embracing change instead of fearing it, and always striving for growth and improvement.

Here's how you can embrace the entrepreneurial mindset:

01. Embrace Uncertainty and Risk

Entrepreneurship is inherently risky and uncertain. Rather than fearing these elements, embrace them as part of the journey. Develop a healthy relationship with risk, seeing it as a necessary part of success, rather than something to avoid.

02. Cultivate Resilience

There will be challenges and setbacks on your entrepreneurial journey. Cultivating resilience—the ability to bounce back from adversity—will help you to navigate these obstacles and keep moving forward.

03. Practice Creativity and Innovation

Entrepreneurs are innovators. They think outside the box and aren't afraid to break the mold. Make a habit of challenging the status quo and looking for unique solutions to problems.

04. Develop a Growth Mindset

A growth mindset, as opposed to a fixed mindset, sees abilities and intelligence as qualities that can be developed with effort and persistence. Believe in your ability to learn, grow, and improve.

05. Focus on Creating Value

Entrepreneurs are value creators. They're not just interested in making money; they want to make a difference. Keep your focus on the value you can create for your customers, employees, and community.

06. Foster a Long-Term Vision

Entrepreneurs are visionaries. They look beyond the immediate challenges and keep their eyes on the bigger picture. Cultivate the ability to set long-term goals and stay focused on them, even in the face of short-term setbacks.

07. Be Persistent

Persistence is key to entrepreneurial success. There will be times when you feel like giving up, but it's important to keep pushing forward. Understand that every challenge is a learning opportunity and a step closer to your goal.

08. Stay Curious

Entrepreneurs are lifelong learners. They are curious, open-minded, and always eager to learn new things. Cultivate your curiosity and make learning a lifelong habit. Embracing the entrepreneurial mindset is about more than just starting a business—it's about adopting a new way of thinking and living. It's about embracing uncertainty, focusing on growth, and always striving to create value. It's not always easy, but it's an incredibly rewarding journey that can lead to personal growth, success, and a meaningful impact on the world.

PART 01:

Finding Your 'Why'
The Importance of Passion

PART 02:

Finding Your 'Why'
Defining Your Purpose

Chapter 2:
Finding Your 'Why'
The Importance of Passion

Passion is the fuel that drives entrepreneurs. It's the deep, burning desire to create, to solve problems, to make a difference. It's what gets you up in the morning, keeps you working late into the night, and propels you through the inevitable challenges and setbacks you'll face on your entrepreneurial journey.

Here are a few reasons why passion is so important in entrepreneurship:

01. Passion Fuels Perseverance

Entrepreneurship is a marathon, not a sprint. It requires a tremendous amount of effort and endurance. Passion for your work gives you the energy and determination to keep going, even when things get tough.

02. Passion Inspires Others

Passion is contagious. When you're genuinely excited and passionate about what you do, it inspires others – your team, your customers, your investors – to believe in your vision and join you on your journey.

03. Passion Enhances Creativity

When you're passionate about something, you're naturally more engaged and invested. This can enhance your creativity and lead to more innovative ideas and solutions.

04. Passion Leads to Excellence

Passionate entrepreneurs are not content with mediocrity. They strive for excellence in everything they do, and this commitment to quality can be a significant factor in their success.

05. Passion Helps Overcome Fear

Starting a business can be scary. There are risks and uncertainties, and the fear of failure is very real. But when you're passionate about what you do, that passion can help you overcome your fears and take the leap into entrepreneurship.

While passion is not the only factor in entrepreneurial success – you also need a viable business idea, a solid business plan, and a lot of hard work – it is a vital ingredient. It's what drives you, what sustains you, and what ultimately helps you to create something meaningful and impactful. So, as you embark on your entrepreneurial journey, make sure to find and follow your passion. It will light your way and keep you going even in the darkest times.

Chapter 2:
Finding Your 'Why'
Defining Your Purpose

Just as passion is the fuel that drives you, purpose is the compass that guides you on your entrepreneurial journey. Your purpose – your 'why' – is the reason you're embarking on this journey. It's the underlying goal that motivates and inspires you and gives meaning to your work. Finding your purpose is not always easy, but it's an essential step in becoming a successful entrepreneur.

Here's a step-by-step guide to help you define your purpose:

01. Reflect on Your Passions and Interests

What do you love doing? What topics or activities make you lose track of time? What would you do even if you weren't getting paid for it? Reflecting on these questions can help you identify potential areas of purpose.

02. Identify Your Strengths

What are you naturally good at? What skills have you developed over time? Identifying your strengths can help you determine how you might be able to create value and make a difference.

03. Consider Your Experiences

Your experiences – both personal and professional – can play a big role in shaping your purpose. What experiences have had a significant impact on you? What lessons have you learned? Reflecting on these experiences can provide valuable insights into what truly matters to you.

04. Identify Problems You Want to Solve

Entrepreneurs are problem-solvers. What problems do you see in the world that you'd like to solve? What changes would you like to see? These issues might point towards your purpose.

05. Define Your Values

Your values are the principles that guide your behavior and decisions. They are the core of who you are as a person. What values are most important to you? How do you want your business to reflect those values?

06.Craft Your Purpose Statement:

Once you've reflected on these areas, try to articulate your purpose into a statement. Your purpose statement should express why you do what you do, what impact you want to have, and how you intend to create that impact.

Defining your purpose is a deeply personal process, and there's no one-size-fits-all approach. Your purpose will be unique to you, and it may evolve over time as you grow and change.

Having a clear sense of purpose will guide your decisions, keep you focused on your goals, and help you maintain your motivation and commitment throughout your entrepreneurial journey.

Chapter 03

PART 01:

Fueling Your Entrepreneurial Engine Unleashing Your Creativity

PART 02:

Fueling Your Entrepreneurial Engine Harnessing Your Energy and Drive

Chapter 3:
Fueling Your Entrepreneurial Engine Unleashing Your Creativity

Creativity is at the heart of entrepreneurship. It's what allows entrepreneurs to come up with innovative ideas, solve complex problems, and create unique value.

Here are several strategies to help you unleash your creativity:

01. Cultivate a Creative Mindset

Creativity starts in the mind. Foster a mindset that embraces curiosity, encourages questioning, and is open to new ideas and perspectives.

02. Seek Inspiration

Inspiration can come from anywhere, at any time. Engage in a variety of experiences, expose yourself to different cultures, perspectives, and fields of knowledge. These experiences can spark new ideas and insights.

03. Practice Brainstorming

Brainstorming can be a powerful tool for generating creative ideas. Encourage free thinking and withhold judgment during the process to allow for the freest flow of ideas.

04. Embrace Failure and Learn from It

Don't be afraid to make mistakes. Often, the most creative ideas come from trial and error. When something doesn't work out, use it as a learning experience and a steppingstone to your next idea.

05. Find Your Creative Environment

Everyone has a place where they feel most creative, whether it's a quiet room, a bustling café, or a walk-in nature. Find your creative environment and use it to stimulate your thinking.

06. Collaborate with Others

Creativity often flourishes in collaboration. Working with others can expose you to different perspectives and ideas, sparking your own creativity.

07. Take Time for Reflection

Creativity needs time to flourish. Regularly set aside quiet time for reflection and thought. This might involve meditation, journaling, or simply sitting in silence.

08. Take Care of Your Physical Health

Physical health plays a significant role in mental function. Regular exercise, a healthy diet, and plenty of sleep can all contribute to a more creative mind.

Remember, creativity is not a trait that only a few lucky individuals possess. It's a skill that can be cultivated and developed. By implementing these strategies, you can unlock your creative potential and use it to drive your entrepreneurial success.

Chapter 3:
Fueling Your Entrepreneurial Engine Harnessing Your Energy and Drive

Being an entrepreneur requires tremendous energy and drive. It involves long hours, hard work, and the ability to push through challenges and setbacks. Harnessing your energy and drive is crucial for propelling your entrepreneurial endeavors forward.

Here's how you can do it:

01. Set Clear Goals

Goals give direction to your energy and drive. They clarify what you're working towards and help keep you motivated. Make sure your goals are specific, measurable, achievable, relevant, and time-bound (SMART).

02. Practice Self-Discipline

Harnessing your energy and drive involves self-discipline. This includes managing your time effectively, maintaining focus, and sticking to your commitments, even when it's difficult.

03. Cultivate Resilience

Entrepreneurship involves setbacks and failures. Cultivating resilience – the ability to bounce back from adversity – will help you stay driven and keep moving forward.

04. Maintain a Positive Attitude

A positive attitude can keep your energy and drive high. Try to stay optimistic, even in the face of challenges, and look for the silver linings in difficult situations.

05. Take Care of Your Physical Health

Physical health and energy are closely linked. Regular exercise, a healthy diet, and enough sleep can boost your energy levels and enhance your overall drive.

06. Find Your Why

Remembering why you're pursuing entrepreneurship – your purpose and passion – can fuel your drive and help you stay motivated.

07. Practice Self-Care

Entrepreneurship can be stressful, and burnout is a real risk. Regular self-care, including breaks, relaxation, and hobbies can help to replenish your energy and maintain your drive.

08. Stay Curious

Keep your mind engaged and open to new ideas. Lifelong learning can boost your drive and fuel your energy for entrepreneurship.

Harnessing your energy and drive is about much more than just working hard. It's about setting clear goals, maintaining a positive attitude, and taking care of both your physical and mental health. It's about staying resilient, passionate, and curious. When you successfully harness your energy and drive, you'll be well-equipped to navigate the entrepreneurial journey and propel your business towards success.

PART 01:

Overcoming Fear and Doubt Dealing with Uncertainty

PART 02:

Overcoming Fear and Doubt Developing Resilience

Chapter 4:
Overcoming Fear and Doubt
Dealing with Uncertainty

Entrepreneurship is a path filled with uncertainty. Every decision you make, every risk you take, carries with it a degree of uncertainty. Yet, it's this very uncertainty that often leads to great innovation and success.

Here's how you can effectively deal with uncertainty as an entrepreneur:

01. Embrace Uncertainty

The first step in dealing with uncertainty is to accept it as a part of the entrepreneurial journey. Embrace it as an opportunity for growth, learning, and innovation.

02. Trust in Your Abilities

Believe in your ability to navigate uncertain situations. Trust in your skills, your knowledge, and your instincts.

03. Break Down Big Challenges

Large, uncertain situations can feel overwhelming. Breaking them down into smaller, manageable tasks can make them feel more approachable and less stressful.

04. Practice Flexibility

Uncertainty often requires adaptability. Be ready to pivot, adjust your plans, and embrace new opportunities as they arise.

05. Develop a Strong Support Network:

A strong support network can provide emotional support, practical advice, and different perspectives when you're dealing with uncertainty.

06. Use Stress-Management Techniques

Uncertainty can cause stress, but stress can be managed. Techniques such as mindfulness, meditation, and regular exercise can help manage stress levels.

07. Learn from the Past

Look back at times when you've successfully navigated uncertainty in the past. What strategies worked? What did you learn?

08. Make a Plan, but Be Prepared to Deviate

Having a plan provides structure and direction, but it's equally important to be ready to deviate from that plan as situations change and new information emerges.

Uncertainty is not something to be feared, but rather something to be managed and even embraced. By developing the right mindset and strategies, you can effectively navigate the uncertainties of entrepreneurship and use them to your advantage. Remember, it's often in the midst of uncertainty where the greatest opportunities for growth and innovation lie.

Chapter 4:
Overcoming Fear and Doubt Developing Resilience

Resilience, or the ability to recover and bounce back from adversity, is a crucial trait for entrepreneurs. As an entrepreneur, you are guaranteed to face obstacles, setbacks, and even failures. Developing resilience can help you navigate these challenges and come out stronger on the other side.

Here's how you can build your resilience:

01. Cultivate a Growth Mindset

A growth mindset, as coined by psychologist Carol Dweck, is the belief that abilities and intelligence can be developed. When you embrace a growth mindset, you view challenges as opportunities to learn and grow, rather than as insurmountable obstacles.

02. Practice Optimism:

Optimism isn't about ignoring the reality of a situation. It's about choosing to focus on the positive and maintaining the belief that things can improve. Try to look for the silver linings in difficult situations.

03. Build a Strong Support Network

Having people who support and believe in you can be incredibly beneficial for your resilience. This network can provide encouragement, advice, and a fresh perspective when you're facing challenges.

04. Take Care of Your Physical Health

Your physical health can significantly impact your emotional resilience. Regular exercise, a balanced diet, and sufficient sleep can all boost your capacity to handle stress and recover from setbacks.

05. Practice Emotional Intelligence

Emotional intelligence involves understanding and managing your emotions. By becoming more aware of your emotions, you can better navigate the ups and downs of entrepreneurship.

06. Set Realistic Goals

Setting achievable goals gives you a sense of purpose and direction. When you experience setbacks, these goals can provide motivation to keep going.

07. Embrace Failure

Accept that failure is a part of the entrepreneurial journey. Instead of fearing failure, view it as a valuable learning experience.

08. Practice Self-Compassion

Be kind to yourself during tough times. Acknowledge your struggles without judgement and remember that it's okay to make mistakes.

Building resilience takes time, but it's an investment that can pay off immensely on your entrepreneurial journey. By cultivating a growth mindset, practicing optimism, and embracing failure, you can develop the resilience needed to navigate challenges and propel your business forward.

Chapter 05

PART 01:

Overcoming Fear and Doubt Dealing with Uncertainty

PART 02:

Overcoming Fear and Doubt Developing Resilience

Chapter 5:
The Power of Vision Setting Your Sights High

In entrepreneurship, a vision is your imagined future, a picture of what you want to achieve with your business. It provides a roadmap for your journey and serves as a source of inspiration and motivation.

Here are some steps to setting your sights high and defining a strong, inspiring vision for your business:

01. Dream Big

Don't limit your vision to what seems immediately achievable. Dare to dream big. What would you want to achieve with your business if there were no constraints?

02. Align Your Vision with Your Values

Your vision should align with your personal values and beliefs. This alignment will make your vision more compelling and will help to ensure you remain motivated to achieve it.

03. Make it Specific

A clear, specific vision is more powerful than a vague one. Try to define precisely what success looks like for your business.

04. Keep it Future-Focused

A vision is about the future, not the present. Where do you want your business to be in five years? Ten years?

05. Write it Down

Writing your vision down makes it concrete and tangible. It's a constant reminder of what you're working towards.

06. Share Your Vision

Sharing your vision with others can make it more powerful. It can inspire your team, attract investors, and draw in customers who share your vision.

07. Review and Refine

As your business grows and changes, your vision might need to be adjusted. Regularly review your vision and make necessary refinements.

Setting your sights high is about having the courage and audacity to dream big. It's about defining an ambitious, inspiring vision for your business and then working tirelessly to make that vision a reality.

Remember, as an entrepreneur, your vision is your guiding star. It lights your way and keeps you on track towards your ultimate goals.

Chapter 5:
The Power of Vision Setting Your Sights High

In entrepreneurship, a vision is your imagined future, a picture of what you want to achieve with your business. It provides a roadmap for your journey and serves as a source of inspiration and motivation.

Here are some steps to setting your sights high and defining a strong, inspiring vision for your business:

01. Dream Big

Don't limit your vision to what seems immediately achievable. Dare to dream big. What would you want to achieve with your business if there were no constraints?

02. Align Your Vision with Your Values

Your vision should align with your personal values and beliefs. This alignment will make your vision more compelling and will help to ensure you remain motivated to achieve it.

03. Make it Specific

A clear, specific vision is more powerful than a vague one. Try to define precisely what success looks like for your business.

04. Keep it Future-Focused

A vision is about the future, not the present. Where do you want your business to be in five years? Ten years?

05. Write it Down

Writing your vision down makes it concrete and tangible. It's a constant reminder of what you're working towards.

06. Share Your Vision

Sharing your vision with others can make it more powerful. It can inspire your team, attract investors, and draw in customers who share your vision.

07. Review and Refine

As your business grows and changes, your vision might need to be adjusted. Regularly review your vision and make necessary refinements.

Setting your sights high is about having the courage and audacity to dream big. It's about defining an ambitious, inspiring vision for your business and then working tirelessly to make that vision a reality.

Remember, as an entrepreneur, your vision is your guiding star. It lights your way and keeps you on track towards your ultimate goals.

08. Share and Revisit Regularly

Once you're happy with your mission statement, share it with your team, customers, and other stakeholders. Regularly revisit your mission statement to ensure it stays relevant as your business evolves.

A powerful mission statement can serve as a rallying cry that unites and motivates your team. It can also inspire confidence and loyalty in your customers. By clearly defining and communicating your mission, you can help others to see and believe in your vision for your business.

Chapter 06

PART 01:

The Role of Goals in Entrepreneurial Success Goal-Setting 101

PART 02:

The Role of Goals in Entrepreneurial Success Making Your Goals SMART

Chapter 6:
The Role of Goals in Entrepreneurial Success Goal-Setting 101

Setting goals is an integral part of the entrepreneurial journey. Goals provide direction, motivate us, and serve as a benchmark for success.

Here is a basic guide to effective goal setting for entrepreneurs:

01. Align Goals with Vision and Mission

Your goals should align with and support your broader vision and mission. This ensures that all your efforts are moving in the same direction.

02. Be SMART about Your Goals

SMART stands for Specific, Measurable, Achievable, Relevant, and Time-bound. A SMART goal is clear and concrete, and it's something you can realistically achieve within a specified time frame

03. Set Short-Term and Long-Term Goals

Long-term goals provide a vision for the future, while short-term goals offer actionable steps toward that vision. It's important to have a mix of both.

04. Break Down Large Goals

Large, ambitious goals can seem overwhelming. Breaking them down into smaller, more manageable tasks can make them seem less daunting and more achievable.

05. Write Down Your Goals

Writing down your goals makes them real and tangible. It also helps you to commit to them.

06. Regularly Review and Update Your Goals

As your business evolves, your goals may need to change as well. Regularly review your goals and make adjustments as needed.

07. Share Your Goals

Sharing your goals with your team can foster a sense of unity and collective purpose. It can also hold you accountable to your goals.

08. Celebrate Achievements

Celebrating when you achieve a goal can boost morale and motivation. It's important to recognize and appreciate your progress.

Goals provide a roadmap for your entrepreneurial journey. By setting clear, achievable goals that align with your vision and mission, you can stay focused, motivated, and on track towards success.

Remember, the journey to achieving your vision is a series of steps, each represented by a goal. Stay committed to your goals, and you'll move steadily towards your entrepreneurial dreams.

Chapter 6:
The Role of Goals in Entrepreneurial Success Making Your Goals SMART

The SMART framework is a tried-and-true method that can make your goals more clear, focused, and achievable. SMART stands for Specific, Measurable, Achievable, Relevant, and Time-bound.

Here's a breakdown of each component and how to apply it:

01. Specific

Your goals should be clear and specific. Instead of setting a vague goal like "I want to grow my business", you might say, "I want to increase our customer base by 20%."

02. Measurable

For a goal to be measurable, you must be able to track your progress and determine when the goal has been achieved. Using numbers, percentages, or specific milestones can help make your goal measurable.

03. Achievable

While it's good to be ambitious, your goals should also be realistic and attainable. Consider your resources, capabilities, and limitations when setting goals. A goal that is impossible to achieve can be demoralizing and counterproductive.

04. Relevant

Your goals should be aligned with your overall business vision and mission. If a goal doesn't contribute to your broader objectives, it may not be worth pursuing.

05. Time-bound

Setting a deadline for achieving your goal can help motivate you and prompt action.

A time-bound goal might be "I want to increase our customer base by 20% within the next six months."

Let's look at an example of a SMART goal for an entrepreneur: "I want to increase online sales of our product by 30% over the next quarter using targeted digital marketing strategies."

This goal is:

- **Specific**: It clearly identifies what the entrepreneur wants to achieve: a 30% increase in online sales.
- **Measurable**: The increase in sales is quantifiable.
- **Achievable**: Assuming the entrepreneur has the necessary resources and skills, a 30% increase is likely achievable.
- **Relevant**: If the entrepreneur's broader goal is to grow their business, then increasing sales is certainly relevant.
- **Time-bound**: The goal is to achieve the increase over the next quarter.

Making your goals SMART can significantly enhance your focus, motivation, and chances of success. By setting SMART goals, you'll be well-equipped to move your business forward and achieve your entrepreneurial vision.

Chapter 07

PART 01:

Turning Obstacles into Opportunities Embracing Challenges as Stepping-Stones

PART 02:

Turning Obstacles into Opportunities Learning from Failure

Chapter 7: Turning Obstacles into Opportunities Embracing Challenges as Stepping-Stones

As an entrepreneur, challenges are part of your everyday reality. However, the most successful entrepreneurs don't just overcome obstacles; they transform them into opportunities for growth and innovation.

Here's how you can start viewing and embracing challenges as stepping stones:

01. Shift Your Mindset

Begin by changing the way you perceive challenges. Instead of viewing them as roadblocks, see them as opportunities to learn, adapt, and improve.

02. Find the Learning Opportunity

Every challenge presents a chance to learn. Ask yourself, "What can I learn from this situation?" This could be a lesson about your business, your market, or even about yourself as a leader.

03. Leverage Your Creativity

Challenges often require creative solutions. Use obstacles as a chance to think outside the box and come up with innovative ideas.

04. Build Resilience

Each challenge you face and overcome makes you stronger and more resilient. Remember this when you're facing a particularly tough obstacle.

05. Ask for Help

You don't have to face challenges alone. Lean on your team, mentors, or other entrepreneurs. They can provide different perspectives and potential solutions.

06. Keep the Big Picture in Mind

Don't get so bogged down in the challenge that you lose sight of your broader vision and goals. Keep them in mind to stay motivated and on track.

07. Celebrate Your Wins

When you successfully navigate a challenge, take the time to celebrate. This not only boosts morale but also reinforces your capability to overcome obstacles.

Remember, entrepreneurship is a journey fraught with challenges. By embracing these challenges as steppingstones, you'll not only overcome them, but you'll also grow and evolve as an entrepreneur.

Challenges are what shape and refine us, helping us to become more resilient, creative, and successful. So, the next time you face a challenge, don't shy away from it. Embrace it, learn from it, and use it as a steppingstone to greater success.

Chapter 7:
Turning Obstacles into Opportunities Learning from Failure

01. Normalize Failure
First, understand that failure is a natural part of the entrepreneurial journey. It's not a reflection of your worth or potential. Even the most successful entrepreneurs have faced failure.

02. Reflect and Analyze
When a failure occurs, take the time to reflect on what went wrong. Were there warning signs? Could different decisions have been made? This analysis can provide valuable insights for the future.

03. Identify Lessons
Failure offers rich learning opportunities. What can you take away from this experience that can help you moving forward?

04. Adapt and Improve
Use your newfound insights to make changes in your strategies, operations, or decision-making processes. This is how growth happens.

05. Practice Resilience
Pick yourself up and keep going. Resilience is a key trait of successful entrepreneurs.

06. Maintain a Growth Mindset
As Carol Dweck's concept suggests, view failure not as a dead-end, but as a stepping stone to progress. You haven't failed - you've found a way that doesn't work.

07. Share Your Experience

Don't hide your failures. By sharing your experiences with others, you can cultivate a culture that values learning and growth over perfection.

In the world of entrepreneurship, failure can be a powerful catalyst for growth. Embrace it, learn from it, and let it propel you forward. Remember, every failure brings you one step closer to success.

As Thomas Edison once said, "I have not failed. I've just found 10,000 ways that won't work." This spirit of perseverance and determination in the face of failure is the essence of entrepreneurship.

Chapter 08

PART 01:

**Building Your Entrepreneurial Tribe
Finding Your Support Network**

PART 02:

**Building Your Entrepreneurial Tribe
Inspiring Your Team**

Chapter 8:
Building Your Entrepreneurial Tribe Finding Your Support Network

The entrepreneurial journey is often depicted as a solitary one, but this doesn't have to be the case. Building a solid support network can make the journey less challenging and more rewarding.

Here's how to find your entrepreneurial tribe:

01. Surround Yourself with Positive Influence

Choose to be around people who inspire, support, and challenge you. Positive energy is contagious, and so is negativity. Make sure you're getting influenced by the right kind.

02. Join Entrepreneurial Networks

There are numerous networks and communities for entrepreneurs, both online and offline. These can be excellent sources of advice, inspiration, and opportunities.

03. Find Mentors and Advisors

These are individuals who have experience and wisdom to share. A good mentor can provide guidance, keep you grounded, and help you navigate the business landscape.

04. Connect with Peers

Other entrepreneurs can be a source of comfort and understanding. They're going through the same journey and can offer unique insights and empathy.

05. Build a Strong Team

Your employees are a crucial part of your support network. Invest time and energy in hiring people who share your vision and passion.

06. Cultivate Relationships with Stakeholders

This includes your customers, investors, and suppliers. These relationships can offer invaluable support in various ways.

07. Don't Forget Your Personal Relationships

Your family and friends can provide emotional support, perspective, and a necessary escape from the pressures of entrepreneurship.

Building your entrepreneurial tribe doesn't happen overnight. It requires time, effort, and genuine relationship-building. But the rewards are well worth it. With a strong support network, you'll be better equipped to face the challenges of entrepreneurship and to celebrate the successes.

Chapter 8:
Building Your Entrepreneurial Tribe Inspiring Your Team

A motivated and inspired team can be your greatest asset as an entrepreneur.

Here's how you can inspire and energize your team:

01. Share Your Vision

Be transparent about your goals and aspirations for the business. Make your team feel part of something larger, and they will be more motivated to contribute to that vision.

02. Lead by Example

Demonstrate the values, work ethic, and dedication that you want your team to emulate. Your actions will influence your team more than your words.

03. Encourage Professional Growth

Provide opportunities for learning and development. When your team members see a chance to grow and advance, they are more likely to stay motivated and committed.

04. Show Appreciation

Regularly acknowledge and appreciate your team's efforts and accomplishments. A simple thank you can go a long way in boosting morale.

05. Foster a Positive Work Environment

Create a culture that values collaboration, creativity, and open communication. An inspiring work environment can greatly enhance productivity and satisfaction.

06. Empower Your Team

Give your team members the autonomy and trust to do their jobs. Empowered employees are often more engaged, creative, and loyal.

07. Communicate Effectively

Keep your team in the loop about what's happening in the business. Regular, transparent communication can prevent misunderstandings and promote a sense of unity.

08. Handle Failures Positively

Show your team that it's okay to make mistakes and that failures are opportunities to learn and grow.

Remember, inspiring your team isn't about grand gestures or motivational speeches. It's about creating an environment where they can grow, thrive, and feel valued. An inspired team can propel your business towards its vision faster than anything else.

Chapter 09

PART 01:

Continuous Learning and Growth
Embracing Lifelong Learning

PART 02:

Continuous Learning and Growth
Staying Current in Your Field

Chapter 9:
Continuous Learning and Growth Embracing Lifelong Learning

In a rapidly evolving business world, the ability to continuously learn and adapt is critical. As an entrepreneur, you must commit to being a lifelong learner.

Here's how you can embrace and foster a culture of continuous learning:

01. Cultivate Curiosity

Be open-minded and curious about the world around you. Ask questions, seek answers, and strive to understand things on a deeper level.

02. Stay Updated

Keep abreast of the latest trends, developments, and ideas in your industry. This could be through reading articles, attending seminars, or subscribing to industry newsletters.

03. Learn from Others

Leverage the knowledge and experiences of others. This could be through mentoring relationships, networking events, or simply having conversations with a diverse range of people.

04. Encourage Learning in Your Team

Promote a culture of learning within your organization. Provide opportunities for training, encourage knowledge sharing, and celebrate learning.

05. Experiment and Take Risks

Don't be afraid to try new things and learn from the outcomes. Even if you fail, there are valuable lessons to be learned.

06. Reflect Regularly

Take time to reflect on your experiences and what you've learned from them. Reflection can yield powerful insights and deepen your learning.

07. Commit to Personal Development

Learning isn't just about professional skills. It's also about personal growth. Invest time in learning new things about yourself, improving your emotional intelligence, and developing your strengths. As the world changes and evolves, so too must entrepreneurs.

By embracing lifelong learning, you ensure that you're always growing, adapting, and staying ahead of the curve. Remember, learning is an investment that always pays off. So, keep learning, keep growing, and keep pushing the boundaries of what you can achieve.

Chapter 9:
Continuous Learning and Growth Staying Current in Your Field

In the fast-paced world of entrepreneurship, staying current in your field is crucial for maintaining a competitive edge.

Here's how you can ensure that you're up-to-date and at the forefront of your industry:

01. Regularly Read Industry News

Subscribe to industry newsletters, follow relevant blogs, and regularly read publications related to your field. This is an easy way to stay aware of trends, advancements, and important events.

02. Attend Conferences and Workshops

Industry conferences, seminars, and workshops are not only great learning opportunities, but also provide networking benefits. You can gain valuable insights from experts and learn from the experiences and strategies of others in your field.

03. Participate in Professional Networks

Join industry or professional organizations. These provide opportunities for networking, learning, and sometimes, access to exclusive resources and information.

04. Invest in Continuous Education

This could involve taking short courses, attending webinars, or even going back to school. Continued education in your field will help you keep your knowledge and skills sharp.

05. Follow Influential People in Your Field

This could be industry leaders, successful entrepreneurs, or thought leaders. You can learn from their experiences, insights, and perspectives.

06. Utilize Social Media

Platforms like LinkedIn and Twitter can be excellent sources of current information. You can follow industry groups, join discussions, and stay informed about trending topics.

07. Encourage Team Learning

Promote a culture of learning in your organization. Encourage your team to stay current in their respective areas and to share their learnings with others.

By making a commitment to stay current in your field, you're taking a crucial step towards ensuring the longevity and success of your business. Remember, the world of business never stands still - neither should your knowledge and skills. Staying updated isn't just about surviving in your industry; it's about thriving

Chapter 10

PART 01:

Maintaining Balance on the
Entrepreneurial Tightrope

Chapter 10: Maintaining Balance on the Entrepreneurial Tightrope

The Importance of Self-Care

As an entrepreneur, it's easy to fall into the trap of all work and no play. However, neglecting self-care can lead to burnout, decreased productivity, and a host of other issues. Here's why self-care is important and how you can incorporate it into your busy schedule:

01. Why Self-Care Matters

Self-care is not just about physical health; it also encompasses mental and emotional well-being. It helps reduce stress, prevent burnout, improve focus and productivity, enhance relationships, and ultimately contributes to better performance in your business.

02. Physical Health

Regular exercise, a balanced diet, and enough sleep are crucial for maintaining your physical health. They give you the energy to tackle your day-to-day tasks and improve your cognitive functions.

03. Mental Well-being

Activities like meditation, mindfulness, and yoga can help you manage stress and stay mentally balanced. Taking breaks and time off work is also essential to recharge your mind.

04. Emotional Health

Make time for activities that bring you joy and relaxation. This could be anything from reading a book to spending time with loved ones. It's also important to cultivate positive relationships and seek support when you're feeling overwhelmed.

05. Setting Boundaries

Learn to separate your work life from your personal life. Set specific work hours and stick to them. Don't let work encroach on your personal time.

06. Regular Check-ins

Regularly check in with yourself to gauge how you're feeling and whether you need a break. Listen to your body and mind and respond to their needs.

As an entrepreneur, you're your business's most valuable asset. So, take care of yourself as you would any other important asset in your business. Self-care is not a luxury; it's a necessity. Remember, your health and well-being are integral to the success of your entrepreneurial journey.

Chapter 10:
Maintaining Balance on the Entrepreneurial Tightrope

Balancing Work and Life

Maintaining a healthy work-life balance is a challenge faced by many entrepreneurs. Juggling the demands of a growing business with personal needs can feel like walking a tightrope. However, achieving balance is not only possible but crucial for sustained success.

Here's how:

01. Prioritize

Not everything needs your attention all the time. Learn to distinguish between what's urgent and what's important. Prioritizing can help you manage your time effectively and reduce feelings of overwhelm.

02. Delegate

As an entrepreneur, it's easy to fall into the trap of wanting to do everything yourself. However, delegating tasks can free up your time and allow you to focus on strategic aspects of your business. Trust your team and let them handle their responsibilities.

03. Set Boundaries

Communicate your availability to your team, clients, and business partners. Make it clear when you are and aren't available for work-related discussions. Respect your own boundaries to help others respect them too.

04. Schedule Personal Time

Just as you would schedule a business meeting, schedule time for your personal activities. This ensures that you're setting aside time for relaxation, hobbies, family, and friends.

05. Use Technology Wisely

Technology can be a double-edged sword. While it can help streamline your work, it can also blur the line between work and personal time. Use it to enhance productivity, but remember to disconnect when needed.

06. Practice Self-Care

Regular exercise, adequate sleep, and a healthy diet can do wonders for your energy levels and mood. Don't overlook the importance of taking care of your mental health too.

07. Seek Support

Don't hesitate to seek support when you need it. This could be in the form of a mentor, a supportive network, or even professional help.

Achieving work-life balance isn't about equally dividing hours between work and personal life. It's about having the flexibility to focus on what's important at the moment, whether that's your business or your personal life. Remember, the goal is to build a business that fits your life, not a life that fits your business.

Chapter 11

PART 01:

Keeping the Flame Alive Staying Motivated for the Long Haul

PART 02:

Keeping the Flame Alive Looking to the Future: Scaling and Beyond

Chapter 11:
Keeping the Flame Alive
Staying Motivated for the Long Haul

Entrepreneurship is a marathon, not a sprint. It's a journey filled with ups and downs, successes and failures, elation, and despair. Staying motivated for the long haul is not only challenging but crucial to your success.

Here are a few ways to keep the entrepreneurial flame alive:

01. Revisit Your 'Why'

In the midst of daily struggles and challenges, it's easy to lose sight of why you embarked on this journey in the first place. Regularly revisit your purpose and remind yourself of what you're working towards.

02. Celebrate Small Wins

Don't wait for big victories to celebrate. Acknowledge and celebrate small wins along the way. They are the stepping stones to your bigger goals.

03. Stay Curious and Keep Learning

Embrace the mindset of a lifelong learner. The desire to learn and grow can serve as a powerful motivator.

04. Nurture Your Passion

Make time for things you love outside your work. They can recharge your batteries and reignite your passion.

05. Practice Gratitude

Even in the face of challenges, there's always something to be grateful for. Gratitude can shift your focus from what's wrong to what's right, and keep you motivated.

06. Surround Yourself with Positivity

Your environment greatly influences your motivation. Surround yourself with positive, uplifting people who inspire you to keep going.

07. Take Care of Your Health

You cannot perform at your best if you're physically or mentally exhausted. Regular exercise, a healthy diet, and adequate rest can significantly boost your motivation and energy levels.

Remember, entrepreneurship is a journey, and every journey has its highs and lows. The key to staying motivated for the long haul is to keep your eyes on the goal, believe in yourself, and enjoy the ride. You've got this!

Chapter 11:
Keeping the Flame Alive
Looking to the Future: Scaling and Beyond

As you look towards the future of your entrepreneurial journey, it's important to plan for growth. Scaling your business can be both exciting and challenging, requiring a clear vision, strategic planning, and an adaptive mindset. Here are some considerations as you prepare to take your business to the next level:

01. Evaluate Readiness
Before embarking on the journey of scaling, critically assess whether your business is ready. Do you have a stable customer base? A proven business model? The necessary resources?

02. Define Your Vision
Having a clear and compelling vision for your business is crucial. It will guide your scaling efforts and serve as a rallying point for your team.

03. Strategize
Scaling doesn't just happen - it requires strategic planning. This includes identifying potential growth areas, setting clear objectives, and developing a detailed plan to achieve them.

04. Build the Right Team
As your business grows, so too will your team. Invest in hiring talented individuals who share your vision and can drive your business forward.

05. Establish Systems and Processes
Efficient systems and processes can help manage the complexities of a growing business. They can also ensure consistency in product/service quality and customer experience.

06. Adapt to Change
Scaling often involves significant changes - to your role, your team, your operations. Embrace these changes and stay flexible in your approach.

07. Stay Focused on the Customer
As your business expands, don't lose sight of what got you here - your customers. Keep them at the heart of all your decisions.

08. Maintain Financial Prudence
Scaling involves investment, and it's important to maintain financial discipline. Make informed financial decisions to ensure your growth is sustainable.

Remember, scaling is not just about growing bigger; it's about growing better. As you look towards the future, stay committed to your entrepreneurial values and vision. Continue to innovate, learn, and adapt, and you'll be well equipped to navigate the exciting journey of scaling and beyond.

> Entrepreneurship is a journey, not a destination. It's about pushing boundaries, breaking new ground, and constantly learning and growing.

It's not always easy, and there will be challenges and obstacles along the way. But with a strong entrepreneurial mindset, a clear vision, and the right support network, you can overcome any obstacle and achieve your dreams.

Keep your spark alive. Stay curious. Stay motivated. And remember: the world needs your ideas, your passion, and your unique entrepreneurial spirit. So go forth and create, innovate, and make your mark on the world! No matter what, Never stop believing!

About the Author

Dr. Lashonda Wofford is a Women of God, a devoted wife, mother, and grandmother. 13 x international best-selling author, a serial entrepreneur, international motivational speaker, business coach, nationally and international accredited life coach and instructor with a passion for helping others discover their potential and achieve their dreams.

With years of experience building startups from the ground up including a 7-Figure Home Care Business and 6-Figure Coaching and Consulting Business. Dr. Wofford knows what it takes to overcome the challenges of entrepreneurship and keep the flame of motivation alive.
She is a community advocate and personal development partner who encourages all to bet on themselves through her All Bets On Me Facebook platform. Through various pains and struggles, Dr. Wofford has learned how to bet on herself and accomplish her goals despite adversities.

Dr. Wofford is a successful businesswoman of color who breaks the ceilings and creates tables for other women to have the same opportunities as she has. some of Dr. Wofford's noteworthy accomplishments are:

Certified Executive Leadership Coach, Certified Life Recovery Coach, Certified Mental Health Specialist, Certified Transformational Coach and Certified Art Therapy Practitioner.

She is the 2022 ACHI Award Recipient for Public Service. She is a proud member of Mt. Zion AME Zion Church.

Other published best sellers include:

Blessed Not Broken vol.1

Pain Equals Purpose

Igniting Your Purpose

90 Days of Biblical Affirmation For Christian Women In Business

Love Business & Marriage

Becoming Her

MarketPlace Mogul The Real Journey of Entrepreneurship.

Girl Let That Go!

Breaking The Chains; Liberating Our Lineage From Generational Curses.

From Brokenness To Brilliance

Black Diamond Chronicles Vol1

Occupy

all can be purchased on her website:
www.drlashondawofford.com

"The Spark: Igniting Your Entrepreneurial Spirit" - your guide to finding and keeping the motivation necessary to succeed as a new or experienced entrepreneur.

all can be purchased on her website:
www.drlashondawofford.com

AUTHOR'S NOTE

I know what it feels like to be a new entrepreneur—full of vision but overwhelmed by where to begin. You're searching for the right systems, the right strategy, the right answers to pull your dreams out of your head and heart and bring them into reality. You want to do more than build a business—you want to fulfill a calling.

I also know what it feels like to be deep in the grind—when the spark that once ignited your purpose begins to dim. When the fire that once fueled your passion starts flickering under the weight of responsibility, uncertainty, and fatigue. When your success starts to feel like survival, and you wonder if you still have the energy to keep going.

This book was born in both of those places. In the early days of building with hope and hustle, and in the quiet moments of burnout where I had to remind myself of who I am and why I started.

Level Up Motivation for Entrepreneurs isn't just motivation—it's mentorship on the page. It's my heart poured out to every dreamer who's still fighting for their future. It's a reminder that you are not alone, and you are more capable than you think.

My hope is that these pages reignite your belief, sharpen your focus, and give you the push you need to rise again—stronger, wiser, and more aligned with your purpose than ever before.

You were never meant to stay stuck.

You were born to level up.

With purpose and power,

Dr. Lashonda Wofford

LETTER TO THE READER

Dear Reader,

If you've made it to this page, let me first say—thank you. Thank you for showing up for yourself, for daring to dream bigger, and for choosing to walk this journey of growth with courage and conviction.

I wrote this book with you in mind—the entrepreneur who's not just building a business, but building a life that reflects purpose, passion, and legacy. Whether you're still laying your foundation or navigating new levels, my hope is that you've found clarity, encouragement, and a renewed fire for your vision.

You are not behind.

You are not disqualified.

You are being shaped by the process—and your next level is unfolding with every step you take.

Remember: true motivation is not about hype. It's about alignment. When your actions align with your purpose, you don't just work—you lead. You don't just hustle—you build something meaningful.

There will be days when doubt knocks at your door, when things move slower than expected, or when the weight feels too heavy. On those days, I want you to come back to these pages. Revisit your "why." Speak life over your vision. And know that you're not alone in this journey.

Keep going. Keep growing. Keep leveling up.

The world needs what only you can offer.

With gratitude and belief in you,

Dr. Lashonda Wofford

You were built for more—and your business was born to thrive.

Whether you're navigating the highs of success or the valleys of uncertainty, *Level Up Motivation for Entrepreneurs* is the boost you've been waiting for. In this transformative guide, **Dr. Lashonda Wofford**—a multi-certified, award-winning leadership coach, international best-selling author, and purpose-driven entrepreneur—offers power-packed strategies to keep your entrepreneurial fire burning.

With a voice that's both motivational and practical, Dr. Wofford helps you push past mindset blocks, rekindle your vision, and take aligned, purposeful action—day by day. This book will inspire you to silence self-doubt, cultivate confidence, and rise into the next level of your calling.

If you're ready to stop playing small, lead with clarity, and build a legacy-driven business, this is your moment.

Don't just start strong—finish fearless. Level up.

www.ingramcontent.com/pod-product-compliance
Lightning Source LLC
Chambersburg PA
CBHW041134130526
44582CB00028B/112